"In large states public education will always be mediocre, for the same reason that in large kitchens the cooking is usually bad."

—Friedrich Nietzsche

So this is a small book…

As you read this short book of stories, jot down a few notes—or whatever your digital equivalent is—and then decide what you will do differently to enhance your bottom line, the way you lead, or the questions you are asking.

Jack Welch said that, "…an organization's ability to learn, and translate that learning into action rapidly, is the ultimate competitive advantage." Review those notes or digital squiggles that you made and decide what you will do differently, turn it into tasks, put the tasks on your calendar—or digital gizmo—and promise to yourself and someone who will follow up with you that you will perform those activities on those dates. Within a few months, you will have made significant progress!

Have fun and be kind, not nice!

—Todd Ordal, 2012

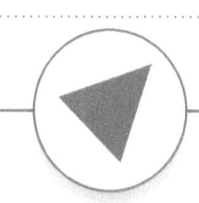

SUCCESSFUL
EXECUTIVES
ARE
NOT NICE!

Missives, Misconceptions
and Other Matters Of
Leadership

by Todd Ordal

APPLIED STRATEGY

Applied Strategy · Boulder, Colorado

www.appliedstrategy.info

ISBN 978-1-300-40559-7

TABLE OF CONTENTS

Nice leaders don't want
anyone to feel bad but,
in the end, many do—
especially the shareholders.

SUCCESSFUL EXECUTIVES ARE NOT NICE!

From the minute we engage with other humans (and even pets!) our parents tell us, "Be nice!" This is intended to be a catchall for don't hit, scream, cry or make someone else feel bad. "Now look at what you did! Little Lisa is crying! Be nice!"

As we get older, we're rewarded for being nice. When my kids were in elementary school, their teachers frequently complimented them for being nice, as in, "He hasn't turned in any of his homework and has failed the past three tests, but he's such a nice boy!"

As adults, we continue to be rewarded for being nice. My wife is nice. When someone knocks on the door trying to sell magazine subscriptions or cookies or trim our trees, she happily has a meaningful conversation with whoever interrupted dinner. Even when she says no, she says it nicely and only after much justification as to why she doesn't need the trees trimmed or another subscription to a magazine full of ads for $6,000 couches.

There isn't much harm in all of this except for lost time and too many Girl Scout cookies in the pantry. However, when we advise or lead and manage others, being nice is ineffective.

There's a substantial difference between being nice ("Don't make Little Lisa cry!") and being kind. In the words of a friend, nice is borne out of fear and kind is borne out of love. Now I'm not going to get all mushy on you (that wouldn't be kind), but he's spot-on. You tell someone you love that he or she is making a big mistake, even at the risk of offending the person.

My wife doesn't want to offend the salesperson, so she sacrifices her time to alleviate any possible rejection on the salesperson's part. However, a key resource that salesperson has is time. Spending inordinate amounts of time with nice people who'll eventually tell you no only after they've gotten to know you is not kind. A kind response might be, "I'm not interested and don't want you to waste your time on me because I'm not purchasing anything."

When my two daughters were still living at home, I could count on them to be kind and tell me that I looked like a nerd when I pulled on some old clothes. I appreciated that. I also appreciate it when someone tells me I look foolish with a piece of spinach in my teeth rather than their hoping it'll come out before I get home and look in the mirror.

Let's take this nice versus kind behavior to the work environment. Nice managers will always find something to compliment. Kind managers will tell you what you need to know to succeed, even when the message is that you're screwing up. Nice leaders don't want anyone to feel bad but, in the end, many do — especially the shareholders. Kind leaders know that leaving weak people on the team means it won't succeed as quickly or as well. Nice leaders don't enforce the rules if someone will get upset. Tardy behavior is allowed and work product is weak because to change behavior would require uncomfortable conversations. Kind leaders know that pushing people to be better, pointing out weaknesses and strengths and having difficult conversations as soon as warranted leads to much more success and, ironically, makes most people happier in the long run. They don't worry so much about the poor performers who can't handle kind and assertive conversations. They kindly escort them out of the company and allow them to find a nice place to settle.

In my work as a strategic adviser to senior executives, I've seen far too much nice behavior cause tremendous problems. Avoiding conflict, allowing weak people to impact others, being nice to vendors who don't deliver, telling board members and senior executives what they want to hear rather than the unvarnished truth — this is not kind behavior. In fact, it destroys value, hampers employment and creates weak performers. Being nice is not kind.

Is your organization nice or kind? Here are some diagnostic questions:

1. Do people speak their minds or hold back because of what others will think?

2. Do weak performers stay employed even though they add no value?

3. If you're the CEO, do you hear about problems before they're catastrophes, or is everything just fine until the doo-doo hits the fan?

4. According to your performance reviews, is your company like Garrison Keillor's Lake Wobegon, where everyone is above average?

5. Have you ever reorganized a department to "work around" an ineffective person?

6. Is healthy conflict not only allowed but also encouraged?

The world is full of nice people, but only kind ones are effective advisors and executives.

"Technology ... the knack of so arranging the world that we don't have to experience it."
—*Max Frisch*

Implementing Strategy
It Starts With 2 Spears

I've been asked several times to recommend the best system for managing strategy implementation. There are many systems you can spend lots of money on to assist with this, but when you don't implement strategy well, you have to look in the mirror.

Imagine that you're a Roman leader in charge of 1,000 somewhat reluctant warriors whom you need to jump into battle concurrently. How do you get them to do this? You grab a spear in each hand and point them at the backs of your top two five-star generals. In turn, they point 2 spears at their top two four-star generals, who each point 2 spears at their three-star generals. This goes on for 10 levels of soldiers until you reach the privates on the front line, 10 levels later. You just need to push slightly on those two spears and a couple of seconds later, all 1,000 jump!

If you don't push the 2 spears in your hands to initiate the sequence, nothing happens! Throwing your spears at the front line is messy and inefficient, and it won't generate much movement.

Fortunately, we now understand that we can gain compliance with spears, but probably not commitment. However, the principal still holds true. Think about accountability meetings rather than spears.

If you're looking for a magic solution to implementing strategy or day-to-day execution that will work without your involvement, good luck. Everything starts at the top, and the system falls apart when there's a weak management layer.

Whether you're the general manager of a business unit or the CEO of a company, you must effectively communicate with your top generals and hold them accountable. They must do the same for the next level; if they can't, you must replace them.

Don't misunderstand me. I'm extremely supportive of collaborative leadership, a compelling vision, positive feedback and strengths-based development. However, these alone won't lead to account-ability throughout the organization. There's no easy "take a pill" so-lution to this.

"One machine can do the work of fifty ordinary men. No machine can do the work of one extraordinary man." —Elbert Hubbard

I originally heard the spear analogy in a conversation with noted author Alan Weiss.

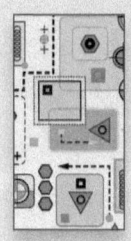

...the system falls apart when

there's a weak management layer.

Did you ask a good question today?

GOOD QUESTION!

Isidor Rabi, a Nobel Prize winning physicist, credited his mother for his interest in science. He described that while other children's parents would ask them what they learned when they came home from school, his mother would ask, "Izzy, did you ask a good question today?"

Someone recently asked me, "Do you think we'd be more successful in market A or market B?" Obviously, I didn't answer with either one. Rather, I asked him five questions:

1. What led you to those two markets?

2. Why do you believe you can prosper in either of those markets?

3. What core competency will you use in those segments?

4. What's the profit potential in those markets?

5. Why are those segments more attractive than exploiting your existing market?

I'm sure you can think of a few more questions, but you get the picture. Sometimes our rush to find an answer doesn't serve us well, particularly when trying to identify business strategy — which I'll define as "how you'll prosper in your environment for some period." Thinking about the "what" (strategy) is much more foreign to most of us than the "how" (tactics). Most business leaders get to their leadership position by being good at tactics and fighting fires. They're promoted to CEO or GM and suddenly are supposed to be good at strategic thinking. What intervention is available to them to allow competency in strategic thinking? When push comes to shove, most will revert to tactics when required to change or reinvigorate strategy.

Tactics without strategy is like flying without a flight plan. It might be fun, but where are you going? To identify strategy, you must ask many questions. At the end of each of your workdays, perhaps you should reflect on what Isidor's mother asked: "Did you ask a good question today?"

Next time you are faced with a problem an opportunity or a decision, ask yourself, "What other questions might be important?" I think that you'll be surprised that the quality of the output is much better when you slow the game down and focus on the quality of the questions before you look for answers.

Try spending more time getting

the questions right and you'll

get better answers.

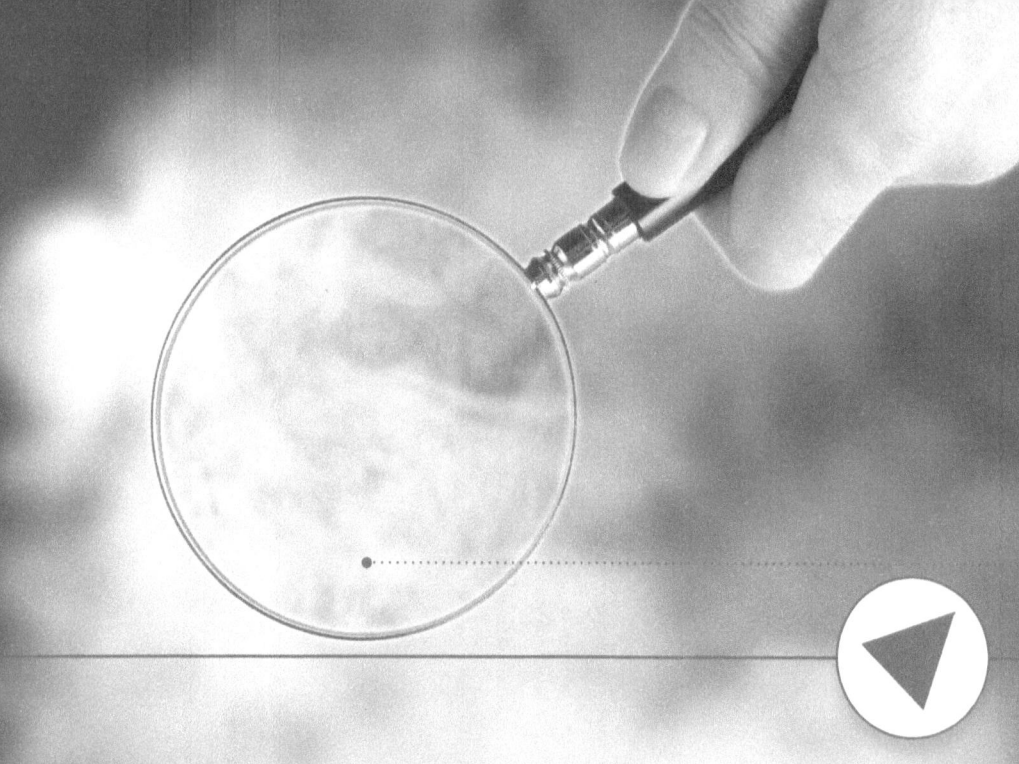

"Neurosis is the inability
to tolerate ambiguity."
—*Sigmund Freud*

AMBIGUITY?
DEAL WITH IT!

Years ago, I was a Kinko's executive in charge of a large part of the country. This was during our rah-rah growth period, and we were opening stores like mad. In preparation for the new year, I put together an expansion plan to open, move and remodel many stores as that was our plan. As you can imagine, this required lots of preparation, resources and time. We ramped up hiring, had our real estate team scurrying like rats on amphetamines, reconfigured operating regions and developed detailed capex plans. The train was in motion. Growth was fun and I was pumped up!

One day our founder, Paul Orfalea, called and out of the blue said something like, "Hey Man, um, we decided not to open all of those stores." What?! I came unglued. Didn't he understand how much work had gone into this planning process? Didn't he understand how many disappointed and pissed off people I was going to have to deal with? Didn't he understand how foolish I was going to look?

Our culture was creative, freewheeling, fun and expressive. It was also full of conflict — some healthy and some not. After I blew off some steam — and Paul was not particularly good at listening to it — the son of a gun chuckled and said, "Toddy Boy, you're just going to have to deal with the ambiguity!" I can still hear him laughing as he hung up the phone. (He even had the nerve to tell this story in his book "Copy This!")

At the time, I was young and full of myself, so I was pretty confident that I was a genius and he was a dope. Now, I'm sure I mixed up the "I" and "he" in that sentence. It was a great lesson to learn. Stuff happens and you can't always eat your alphabet soup A, B, C … Z.

I recently worked with a young executive who was tapped by his CEO as "capable with flaws." As we worked on filling in the gaps, it became evident that he was no better at dealing with ambiguity than I was on that phone call. "Life isn't black and white," I suggested to him. "You need to learn to think in shades of gray." It was so apparent that he'd self-destruct if he couldn't start to identify middle ground and not react with dismay when potholes popped up on his well-planned travel route.

I had to keep this in mind the other night. I called my wife from a business trip and suggested dinner at a specific restaurant at a specific time. I got home that night and we drove to dinner. I skipped a meal on the plane (admittedly just a snack box) and raced home from the airport as my stomach growled. We drove into town and as we approached the restaurant — by this time I'd already mentally ordered a bottle of wine and devoured my main course — she says, "I don't want to go there. I want to go to that new restaurant we talked about." I'm about to blow a fuse when I hear this voice in my head laughing at me and saying, "Toddy Boy, you're just going to have to deal with the ambiguity!" We ended up having a great meal at the restaurant of her choice.

Senior executives must provide clarity for their people yet also deal with ambiguity without going mad. Isn't that ambiguous?!

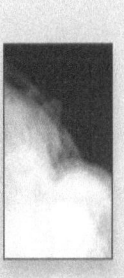

Provide clarity and

deal with the ambiguity.

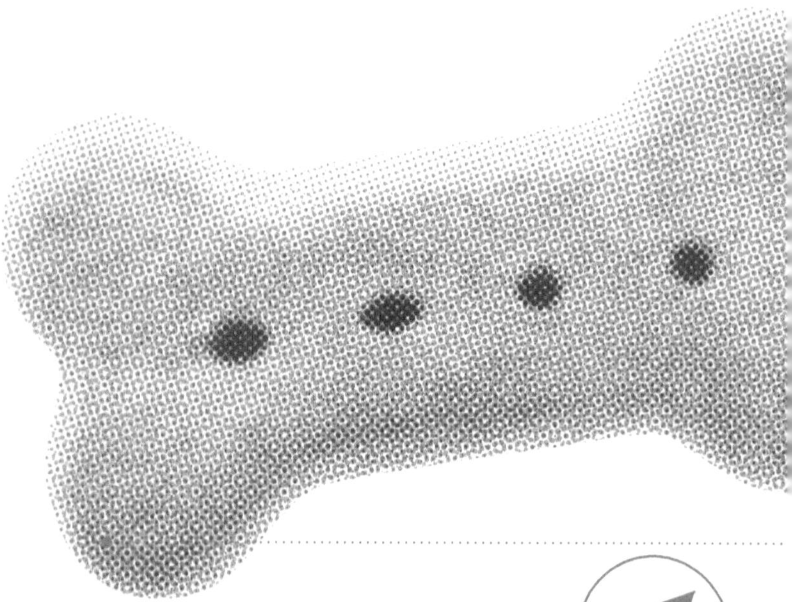

"It is not from the benevolence of the
butcher or the brewer or the baker that
we expect our dinner, but from their
regard to their self-interest."
—Adam Smith, "The Wealth of Nations"

Butchers, Brewers and Bakers...
Loyalty Is
Not Free

I'm always amazed at how many leaders expect people to work against their own self-interest. Some examples: Pitch in on an extra project for no possible reward. Sell new accounts when being paid handsomely for existing revenue. Show initiative when constantly second-guessed. Care about the company's financial performance when treated like a mule and sharing no gain.

Some of these leaders complain that there's no loyalty anymore. There may be some truth to that, but I see it more as an algebraic equation. L (Loyalty) = PR (Perceived Rewards). PRs, however, can mean different things to different people. Several of my kids who are in their 20s are extremely loyal to their employers, but they also get high PRs. One daughter's PR is working with other talented artists, even though her monetary rewards are low. My other daughter gets to work on environmental issues that she's deeply committed to. My son's PR is monetary. If my daughter who works with artists had to work with capitalists like me, she wouldn't be as loyal. (I'm still working on her...) If my other daughter had to work for a smokestack industry, she'd be home on the couch at 5:15 p.m. If my son didn't receive good tips as a bartender, you wouldn't catch him volunteering for another shift when he has an 8 a.m. class.

A few years ago, I met with a CEO who didn't understand why he couldn't get people to come in early or work past 5 p.m. He "couldn't find any good people." He tried mandating longer hours (you can imagine how that went over). He tried hiring new people… repeatedly. He tried tightly monitoring employees' work. However, he didn't try positive feedback, allowing them to come up with their own solutions or sharing any of the large amount of money he made every year — heck, every week! He expected big L with very little PR. In algebraic terms, $L \neq PR$.

Some people have a natural reservoir of L because they expect rewards. They have a positive outlook and bust their tail. I love working with people like that! However, they still need PRs to stay engaged over the long haul. Others tend toward the "show me the money" end of the spectrum and only put out good energy if they see the reward plainly and quickly. If handled correctly, they can be great assets as well.

The invisible hand of self-interest (apologies to Adam Smith) can either guide your actions as a leader or slap you across the face. Make your choice.

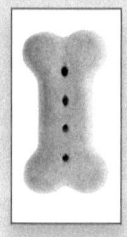

Don't expect people to work

against their self-interest.

True leadership comes with many obligations

IT'S LONELY AT THE TOP

ost CEOs will tell you it's lonely at the top. I was one, and it was. I recently read the book "Managing Change" by Jick and Peiperl. In it, they reproduced a speech by Bob Galvin, the recently deceased former chairman and CEO of Motorola, during what might be described as Motorola's heyday. Here's an excerpt:

"When one is vested with the role of the leader, he inherits more freedom. The power of leadership endows him with the rights to a greater range of self-determination of his own destiny. It is he who may determine the what or the how and the when or the where of important events. Yet, as with all rights, there is a commensurate, balancing group of responsibilities that impose upon his freedom. The leader cannot avoid the act of determining the what or the who and the where. He cannot avoid being prepared to make these de-terminations. He cannot avoid being prepared to make these termi-nations. He cannot avoid living with the consequences of his deci-sion on others and the demands the consequences impose on him. Only time will prove the merit of his stewardship. Because he is driv-en to pass this test of time, he will be obliged often to serve others more than himself. This obligation will more and more circumscribe his destiny. So those who assume true leadership will wonder from time to time if the apparent freedom of the leader adds a greater measure of independence, or whether the dependence of others on him restricts his own freedom."

Many look at CEOs and say, "You lucky bastard …" because they're often very well- compensated and may appear to be "masters of the universe." Many have a good deal of self-confidence, which is sometimes envied and sometimes despised. However, as Galvin eloquently describes, true leadership comes with many obligations and can be quite lonely.

At one point in my life, I was in charge of a 7,000-person organization with $500 million in revenue. It was lots of fun and extremely challenging. However, I wasn't the CEO. My first stint as a CEO was in a 30-person, private-equity-backed turnaround situation. The CEO stint should've been less demanding and easier because it was a much smaller organization. It wasn't. As CEO, you realize (to quote Harry Truman) that "the buck stops here." A lonely spot.

What's the antidote to this loneliness? Four steps.

1. **Mentally create a successful leadership model to work toward.** There are many leadership models, but one of the most simple and effective is from Warren Bennis' article "The Four Competencies of Leadership." I've used this model to successfully advise many senior leaders. The four competencies are attention, meaning, trust and self. To lead others to success, you must have their attention, have winning ideas, gain their trust and be emotionally intelligent.

2. **Get help.** To avoid breathing your own exhaust all day, you need a truth-talker. You won't likely find this person on your staff. It could be a mentor, a group of advisers, a coach or a peer. You need someone who has your best interests at heart but who's

also kind enough to call baloney when he/she sees it, applaud your success and be honest at the risk of offending you.

3. **Develop healthy self-esteem.** Your successes will be due to your effort, many others' effort and a bit of luck. Your failures, and you'll have many, will be attributable to the same list. In other words, lots of things happen to cause failures, and you're only one of them. It doesn't mean you're incompetent.

4. **Lead collaboratively.** You don't have to be the smartest guy in the room; engage others in your quest for success. Led well, a team of people has a cumulative IQ that's much higher than the sum of the individuals.

As Galvin points out, effective leaders cannot avoid determining the organization's direction, making the tough decisions and living with the consequences. They can, however, avoid taking the lonely road.

Power can corrupt and isolate leaders, but it doesn't have to.

Longer
is not better

Return On Time—
The best investment you'll ever make!

"The only reason for time is so that everything doesn't happen at once."
—Albert Einstein

In business, we talk a great deal about "return." Return on investment, cash-on-cash return, return on equity and return on invested capital are a few. However, whether you're a CEO or a sales rep, perhaps your most important measurement of return is your return on time.

Most of you reading this have a good deal of discretion as to how you spend your time. It's unlikely that someone forced you to read this. You decided that at this moment, this is what you should do. (Hint: If this topic has no interest to you, stop now and move on.)

The $59 time-management seminar I went to 30 years ago started off with this statement: "Regardless of who you are, we all have 24 hours in our day." I don't recall anyone jumping up to argue. This obvious point still holds true today. However, we now have 537 cable channels, Facebook, cell phones, email, You Tube and much more traffic to contend with. I watched The Jetsons as a kid and thought about how cool it would be to have all of those gadgets and a robot maid so I'd have more free time. I'm still waiting.

I've worked with many leaders and often had conversations with them about how to best spend their time. As a result, I came up with Todd's Seven Timely Tips for Increasing Return on Time.

1. **Clarify your values.** A great place to start taking control of your time is by identifying your values and then determining whether the activities and time you're investing (or squandering) are consistent with these values. (If you want a vehicle to examine your values, email me and I'll send you a free exercise.)

2. **Be assertive.** You don't need to have a relationship with everybody who rings your doorbell or calls you on the phone. Trying to be nice to everyone prevents you from doing what you should be doing. A talented client who's CEO of a large company recently said, "I don't want to be seen as a jerk, but I just can't go to lunch with everyone who asks." Some will see him as a jerk, but he's right.

3. **Plan.** If you don't plan, how can you know what's most important? If an activity doesn't take you closer to your long-term objectives, do you need to do it, or did you get sidetracked? (It's OK to look at shiny new things occasionally.)

4. **Use "comparative advantage" to your advantage.** (If you aren't familiar with the economics term "comparative advantage," look it up. I swear it'll be a good use of your time.) If you love to mow the lawn, great! If not, get someone who's faster and find a better outlet for your time. I had a client who swore he could do everything better than all of his employees. He probably could, but he was miserable and couldn't grow his business as a result.

5. **Define wealth in terms of discretionary time, not money.** This causes you to think differently about your activities and what has value. The guy above was financially very wealthy but

couldn't take a vacation even though he could afford to buy a jet to do so! I'm writing this on a Monday. I'm skiing tomorrow because there's supposed to be a foot of new snow. (Admittedly, it might be a late night tonight!) Tomorrow, I'll be wealthier than the guy with the pile of money.

6. **Recognize that longer is not better.** Pretend you're hiring me as a consultant to help you solve a large problem. It's going to take six months and require a $250,000 investment, but it will bring in $3 million in new revenue. Wait … I just found a way to do it in five minutes. Does this have more or less value to you? Longer is not better; it's just longer.

7. **Relax.** Nobody gets this right all the time. Just course-correct frequently.

Take five minutes right now to reflect on this and identify what you can do differently to increase your return on time. Do it now!

I hope this provided you a generous return on time.

"…And then one day you find
Ten years have got behind you
No one told you when to run
You missed the starting gun
And you run and you run
To catch up with the sun
But it is sinking…."
—Time, Pink Floyd

Reflection is required

WHITE SPACE

J ust be still!" An investor said this to me years ago when we were awaiting news about our company that would dictate our future. It was good advice.

I'm writing this as I wait for 20 executives to arrive for a senior management meeting that I'm facilitating. Although we have three clear objectives for the conference, there's a strong feeling at this company that any time the group spends together is good time. Conversations are valued more then detailed agendas. Oh, they eventually get around to executing; in fact, planning is one key skill of this leadership team. They are smart enough, however, to understand that more great ideas germinate during the cocktail hour than in tightly structured meetings. By the way, this company produces significant financial results.

When I was an executive at Kinko's, we had an annual meeting called "The Picnic." We flew thousands of people to a beach location such as San Diego or Hawaii to spend a week together. We had a company meeting, some seminars and a vendors' show, but we did the real work on the beach, at the pool or throughout the cocktail hour ... never really relegated to an hour. During those times, real conversations and debates took place about how to grow our business and improve our profitability. Our founder was a genius at understanding that cramming the week full of meetings wasn't a great way to share and learn. He knew that "white space" was the best learning opportunity.

I see far too many executives try to cram 10 pounds of stuff into a 5-pound bag. Eight-hour days become 15-hour days. Agendas are overloaded and rarely finished. Strategic objectives are assembled by the bushel and then reassembled next year because most weren't completed. Meetings are scheduled so tightly you'd think you were in your doctor's office. No time to reflect, think and craft great questions — just a hell-bent-for-leather quest to work more.

As leaders and managers, we don't get paid for activity; we get paid for producing results. More activities don't necessarily produce more results. Have you heard the phrase, "Slow the game down"? It applies to basketball, but it also relates to business. Working quickly is good, but having white space on your calendar, your agenda and your list of strategic objectives is imperative.

Don't cram 10 pounds of stuff

into a 5 pound bag.

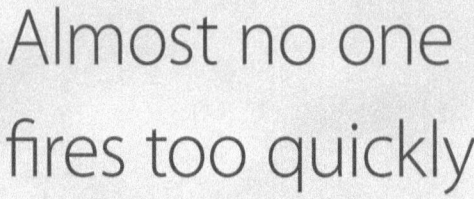

Almost no one
fires too quickly

Hollow on the Inside
Don't create
chocolate bunnies

I recently had coffee with a fraud. He looked good, smelled good, dropped names and used buzzwords like a pro. However, he was a chocolate bunny ... sweet on the outside and hollow on the inside. These characters can deflect blame like a superhero deflects bullets. All fluff and no stuff, they add no value to organizations.

But how do chocolate bunnies evolve? I believe they grow up in organizations with extremely poor leadership, never really held accountable for their actions and results. Perhaps they're even "mentored" by someone who has mastered the art of "nonstick" and is unwittingly passing their skill on to the next generation of bunnies.

When this happens to young businesspeople, they eventually become middle-aged and have no real skills. They are frauds, and it's only partially their fault. When they eventually get into a healthy organization that requires true performance, accountability and emotional intelligence, they fail every time. They often make great strides early because they're gregarious and look good. But once uncovered, they nervously jump from job to job looking for the sanctuary of their early career where being a good guy was enough.

Why bother to write about this? Because leadership positions come with obligations, and one of them is to avoid creating chocolate bunnies. I've worked with senior leaders who are fearful of, or not adept at, holding people accountable. They end up creating a full basket of these bunnies, thereby ruining careers.

So how do you avoid creating chocolate bunnies? Here are four rules that should help:

1. **Avoid the "nice versus kind" trap.** It's nice to avoid conflict and only give people positive feedback, but it's not kind.

2. **Fire faster.** Gosh, that doesn't sound nice, does it? I have yet to meet the leader who says that he or she has been too quick to pull the trigger on nonperformers.

3. **Focus on value.** How does each person on your team add value to the organization? Ask them. If they don't add value but they have talent, help them re-create their job.

4. **Plan and review.** People who execute a meaningful plan with specific objectives tied to the organization's global strategy cannot turn into chocolate bunnies.

I once had a young friend who made good money in a "cushy" job. However, he had no real responsibilities, and leadership in his organization could kindly be described as milquetoast. He was on cruise control but was smart enough to know that he was turning into a chocolate bunny. So he re-created himself in another company and is now successful in a senior position.

Are you creating chocolate bunnies in your organization?

Chocolate bunnies are made,

not born.

Lead,
don't preside

Effective Leaders Must Be Forceful!

I was recently involved in a conversation about culture with a leader who was in a situation requiring significant change. Someone espoused what I would call passive leadership, and I took issue with this. Leadership is not about just presiding — unless, of course, you aspire to be the Queen of England!

A frequently used distinction between management and leadership says that management requires organizing complexity and leadership drives change. If so, then leaders must be forceful! Let me explain my logic.

Force is any influence that causes an object to undergo a change in speed, direction or shape. (I was a psychology major, but my engineer daughter confirmed this.) When you lead an organization (by the definition above), you must use force because you're speeding up, slowing down, adjusting your direction, or changing the shape of your company, product, service or market.

How much force? It depends on how stuck or heavy the company is, how fast and far you want to go or how misshapen you are.

Some leaders are capable of much more force than others. In my experience, those who have tremendous capacity to generate force cannot sit idle or work in static conditions. They're like a Ferrari® on a gravel road. Need very little change? You don't need a forceful leader. Need a lot of change? You need a leader capable of generating lots of force. (Turn-around specialists are of this ilk.)

Force in an organization can be generated in several ways. It can be generated by one large engine or many engines (that is, by engaging your entire team in the effort). It's a bit like one large computer versus massive parallel processing.

My counsel to the "passive" leader who found himself in a situation requiring significant change? Fire up his engine, engage his people and be forceful. Although being forceful generates heat and uses energy, it's the fastest way to change speed, direction and shape.

The more firmly you are stuck,

the more force you must use.

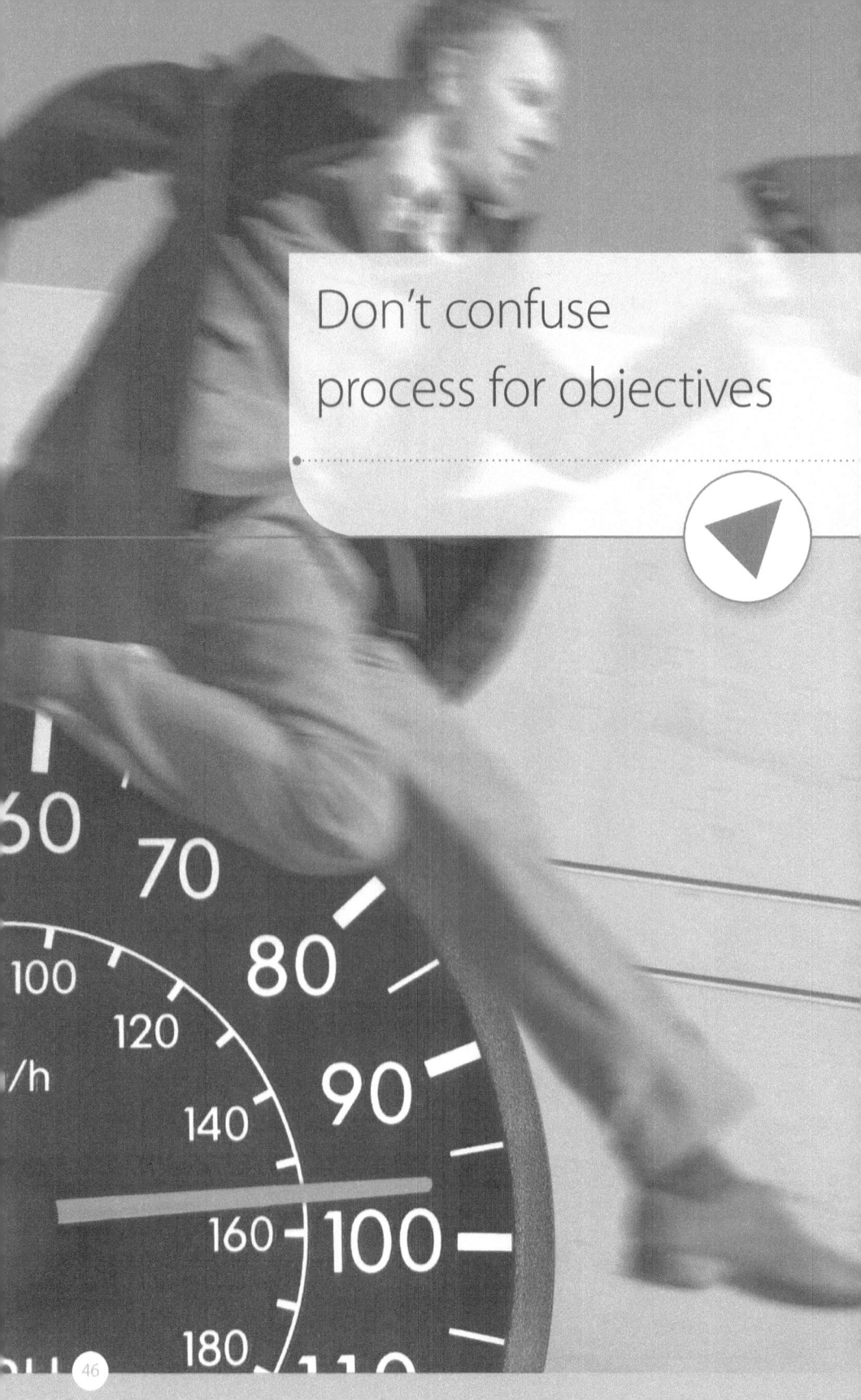

Don't confuse
process for objectives

THE NEED FOR SPEED

One Friday years ago, I called a friend who was a marketing manager at a large company to see if he wanted to have a beer after work. I asked him about his week, and he reported that he'd spent it designing a one-page brochure (if you're under 25, that's a piece of paper). An entire week! And that was before it went to the graphic designers. I was flabbergasted. I'm all for quality and proofreading, but one page in a week?

Speed is often a significant advantage. Faster to market, less executive time, higher ROI. However, we often get caught up in our perceptions about how long something should take. Another friend who's the CEO of a large organization wanted some software written to solve a problem. His internal team of 300 told him it would take a year. He got it done in a week by posting a requirements document on the web and taking bids. Clearly, too many projects in the system can also cause this problem. In this case, however, it was more likely about a free-market solution versus a centrally controlled environment.

I've seen three major impediments to speed in organizational performance.

First, we often confuse process with objectives. They're significantly different. For instance, I sometimes get calls from people who want me to facilitate an "off-site strategic planning meeting." When I ask why, I often find that the real objective is: a) to fill time, b) to continue with the tradition, c) to entertain the troops or d) unknown. Not one of those is a good reason. When I pursued a line of questioning recently with an executive who initially wanted a "strategic planning session," the need I uncovered had to do with a companywide lack of accountability, which required a different solution. If you first clearly identify the objective by asking hard questions, you can then determine how to address the issue most effectively. Ask "what" first, then "how." Unclear objectives will slow you down dramatically.

Second, assumptions slow you down. You can often achieve the objective (notice I didn't say "the most elegant solution") much more quickly than your initial assumption. It's helpful to ask, "What if we had to do this in 10% of the time we allocated?" Once you survive the initial incredulous looks, you just might come up with some very unique answers and save a lot of time.

Last, it's about success, not perfection. Oftentimes, squeezing out the last 10% of a project can take an inordinate amount of resources and time with little or no increase in quality. Clearly define the objective and meet it. When someone asks you to repaint the Sistine Chapel and improve the quality … then you can take your time!

Get fast and get real.

What should you
recycle next week?

WASHING TINFOIL

I recently came home late from a long day hoping I might be graced with leftovers for dinner. Unfortunately, my wife was gone and frankly, her idea of leftovers is the last half of a bag of popcorn anyway (she comes from a long line of culinary-impaired Irish Catholics). As I pulled a pan out to make a rib-sticking concoction, I noticed something that I've seen before that always makes me laugh — a piece of very ragged, used tinfoil that my wife had washed.

I get the "reuse" thing. I resole my dress shoes. I buy into recycling. Hell, in college I used to have my brother — a gearhead who always had nice vehicles — save his used oil so I could pour it into my 1968 Chevy Malibu that got about 10 miles per gallon … of oil, that is, not gas! However, taking the time to wash crumpled, torn, stained tinfoil strikes me as a bit outlandish.

As I contemplated this spotless tinfoil, I thought of a recent meeting I had with a CEO about one of his team members who was clearly a misfit. Coaching, warnings, mentoring, cajoling, training and screaming hadn't had the desired effect. The CEO was washing tinfoil. Sometimes the recycle bin is your best option for bad ideas and bad employees. No intent to be caustic, but start next week by asking yourself, "What ideas or people am I carrying around that should be recycled?"

Don't forget to take out the trash.

Yippee Ki Yay!
Cowboy Wisdom in the Business World

A friend sent me an e-mail the other day with some quotes from Will Rogers. My father-in-law used to say things like, "Let's mount up!" when we were supposed to get in the car to go to dinner, so it struck a chord with me. After rereading it today — it's one of those e-mails that I couldn't seem to delete — I realized that many have business implications. I hope you do too.

1. "Never slap a man who's chewing tobacco" and its close cousin, "Never kick a cow chip on a hot day." Business translation: Think about unintended consequences before you act.

2. "Never miss a good chance to shut up." I've had much better results (a) getting to know people and (b) learning things by asking questions rather than talking. The other day I actually said to a guy, "OK, enough about you; let's talk about me!" after he droned on for about 20 minutes.

3. "Always drink upstream from the herd." Have you ever found yourself hanging around the water cooler with a bunch of people with lots to bitch about but no solutions? Head upstream!

4. "Good judgment comes from experience, and a lot of that

comes from bad judgment." True leaders aren't afraid of making mistakes, and failing fast is a good skill set. An old boss from many years ago said, "You'll never get rich running scared! Make some mistakes!"

5. "If you're riding ahead of the herd, take a look back every now and then to make sure it's still there." The other day, I met with a bright CEO who was a great strategic thinker. His challenge? Slowing down so that everyone else could catch up. In business, the whole team needs to get across the goal line.

6. "If you find yourself in a hole, stop digging." You're running a company or division and your results stink. Do you dig faster or dig elsewhere? It's not always an easy decision. Consider getting some fresh eyes on the problem.

7. "There are three kinds of men: the ones that learn by reading, the few who learn by observation and the rest of them have to pee on the electric fence and find out for themselves." (Note: There are probably three kinds of women as well. …) A few years ago while skiing in Whistler, British Columbia, some friends and I saw a young Australian guy named Angus jump off a very large rock. The result? Big-time yard sale. (By the way, I know his name because I helped him collect his gear and limbs.) We then watched his three buddies all do the same thing with identical results; I guess the fourth guy must have been dumbest. Experiential learning is great, but there's a lot to learn from observation, and it's much less painful (this is often called "best practices" in the business world).

8. "Long ago, when men cursed and beat the ground with sticks, it was called witchcraft. Today it's called golf." No business application, but because I golf about as well as I sing, I liked it.

If you are not learning from others,

expect a few shocks.

Spend time together
and get better results

BUSINESS IS JUST LIKE HIGH SCHOOL

M eryl Streep once famously remarked in a commencement address to college students: *"You have been told that real life is not like college, and you have been correctly informed. Real life is more like high school."*

Remember the important stuff you used to worry about in high school, such as where you sat, with whom you sat, what you wore and how confident you appeared when you tried to talk to girls? Now you're 40 or 50 and a business executive, and guess what? Nothing changed! Oh, you probably don't worry about acne anymore, but the rules of the lunchroom still prevail.

I help executives succeed, and some of that consists of technical skills such as strategic planning, organizational structure design and financial acumen. However, more of it involves "lunchroom" issues such as communicating clearly, deciding with whom and where you spend your time, learning to engage in healthy conflict, developing confidence, solving problems and determining how to do your homework without pulling all-nighters!

Sometimes the behavior that got you into trouble in high school, if directed appropriately, can actually be helpful in the work environment. Remember the brainiac kids from high school whom you were always jealous of? Many of them didn't learn the emotional intelligence skills or appropriate risk taking to succeed in executive suites and are crunching numbers in a cubicle. (The combination of IQ and EQ, however, is what took a few of them to positions of greatness — not always associated with a title.)

I worked with Paul Orfalea, the founder of Kinko's, for quite a few years. He would frequently say, "The A students work for the B students. The C students run the company, and the D students dedicate the buildings." (As a D student, he went on to dedicate a few buildings!) Like Steve Jobs, Paul was prone to bending reality, but the point of his story is sometimes true. High school behavior often carries the day. When you're 50 and running an organization, no one gives a hoot whether you remember the symbol for xenon on the periodic table. (I had to look it up … it's XE.)

Recent work by some MIT and Harvard folks point out that there is real bottom line impact in getting your people to interact more frequently in the lunchroom. It turns out that the companies where people actually spend time together (yes, face-to-face) get better bottom-line results.

So put away your iPhone for a minute. Don't send that text. Don't update Facebook. Go find a human being to talk to in the lunchroom.

Talk is cheap . . . and effective.

ABOUT THE AUTHOR

Todd Ordal, President of Applied Strategy LLC, works as a thought-partner to CEOs and their senior teams to enhance organizational performance through better strategy and effective leadership. He is a former CEO with 32 years of leadership experience and is also a Certified Management Consultant™ and a certified executive coach.

Applied Strategy • Boulder, Colorado

www.appliedstrategy.info

www.ingramcontent.com/pod-product-compliance
Lightning Source LLC
Chambersburg PA
CBHW021916170526
45157CB00005B/2083